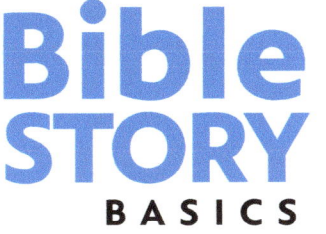

Reader Bible Story Leaflets **SUMMER Year 1**

Bible Story Basics: Building a Better World Through God's Story

Hello!

You're holding in your hands the BIBLE STORY BASICS: READER, BIBLE STORY LEAFLETS. These leaflets help you and your children tell the Bible story in ways they will understand. These leaflets are helpful for in-classroom learning, and they serve as take-home leaflets for families.

Each story has an element to engage your children actively. It might be through a debate or skit, or it might be by empathizing with a particular Bible character. The stories are designed to engage your children through multiple learning styles, in order to build a foundation that will last a lifetime.

These leaflets also encourage parents and caregivers to continue learning about the Bible story at home throughout the week, using the suggestions provided—at family dinners, in the car, and at bedtime.

We hope that you'll find the Bible Story Basics Leaflets helpful as you minister to your children and share God's love with these precious children of God.

Nancy Speas, Bible Story Basics Writer

TO FIND OUT MORE, visit
biblestorybasics.com.

Summer Year 1
Table of Contents

Session 1..........................Paul's Conversion
Parent Take-Home.......Summer Faith Fun
Session 2..........................Love in Action
Session 3..........................Paul Escapes
Session 4..........................Be Glad and Endure
Session 5..........................Be a Leader
Session 6..........................Be Encouraged
Session 7..........................Lydia
Session 8..........................Paul and Silas
Session 9..........................Elijah and the Ravens
Session 10........................Elijah and the Prophets
Session 11........................Elijah and Elisha
Session 12........................Elisha and the Widow
Session 13........................Elisha and Naaman
Unit 1 Bible Verse Take-Home
Unit 2 Bible Verse Take-Home
Unit 3 Bible Verse Take-Home
Bible Library Take-Home

Changes

Changes on the outside are easy to see. Changes on the inside, like Paul's big change, are not. Circle all the changes you see between the first and second pictures.

Talk About It

Use these questions to talk about today's Bible story with your child.

- How do you think Ananias got the courage to go to Paul?
- Have you or somebody you know gone through a big change like Paul did?

PRAY: Thank you, God, for always giving us a chance to change. Amen.

Reader • **Session 1** • Summer Year 1

Paul's Conversion
Acts 9:1-20

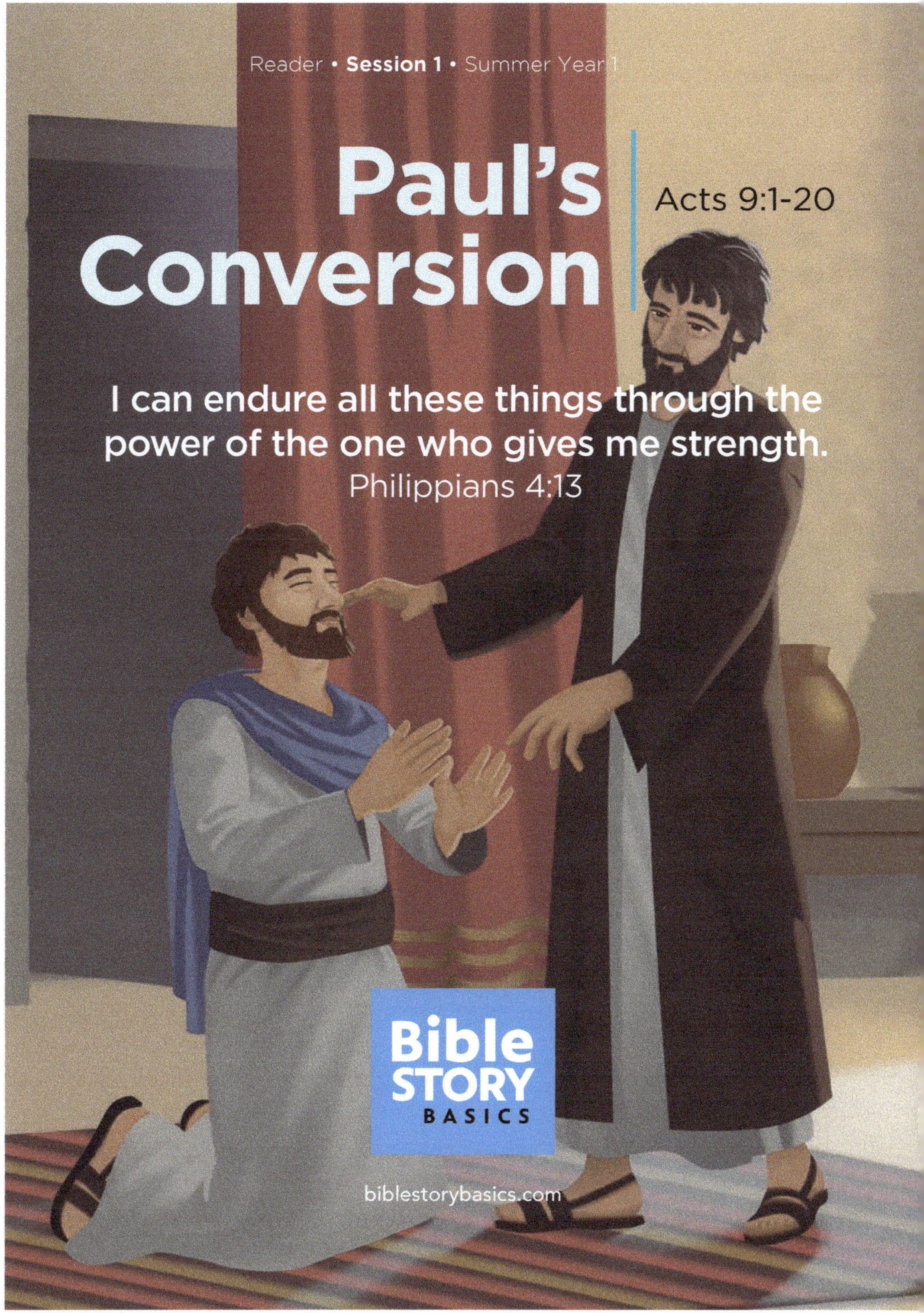

I can endure all these things through the power of the one who gives me strength.
Philippians 4:13

Bible STORY BASICS

biblestorybasics.com

Paul's Conversion

Characters: Narrator, Jesus, Paul, Paul's Friends, Ananias, Bright Light

Narrator: Paul and his friends were on their way to a city called Damascus. *(Paul and Paul's Friends walk down the road.)* Paul had heard that many followers of Jesus were there.

Paul: All followers of Jesus should be put in jail! I'm going to arrest all the Christians and take them back to Jerusalem!

Paul's Friends: Yeah! Let's arrest them!

Narrator: Suddenly, a bright light from heaven flashed around Paul! *(A bright light appears, and Paul jumps in surprise.)* He fell to the ground and covered his eyes. *(Paul falls down.)*

Jesus: Paul! This is Jesus. Why are you being unkind to my followers?

Narrator: *(gasps)* The voice Paul heard was Jesus!

Jesus: Get up and go into the city. Someone will come and help you.

Narrator: Paul stood up. He opened his eyes, but he couldn't see!

Paul: Help me, friends! Paul's friends had to lead Paul into the city of Damascus. *(Paul's Friends lead him down the road.)*

Narrator: Meanwhile, a man named Ananias lived in the city. He was a follower of Jesus.

Jesus: Ananias! Go find Paul. He needs your help.

Ananias: Jesus, is that you? You want me to find Paul? But he'll kill me!

Jesus: You must go to Paul. Go!

Narrator: Even though he was afraid, Ananias went to find Paul. *(Ananias walks over to Paul.)* Paul was sitting in the house. He still could not see.

Ananias: *(shaking)* Paul, please don't kill me. Jesus sent me to help you. *(Ananias touches Paul.)*

Narrator: Immediately, Paul was able to see again!

Paul: *(Jumps in surprise.)* I can see! I am changed! Quick, somebody baptize me! I want to preach about Jesus!

Narrator: Paul was baptized and became a follower of Jesus. Instead of arresting Jesus' followers, Paul became one. The rest is history.

Sunshine, Fun Times

Find and circle the summer travel items hidden in the picture.

Talk About It

Use these questions to talk about your summers with your child.

- What are some of your favorite summer memories?
- What do you hope we can do together as a family this summer?

PRAY: Dear God, thank you for the gift of summer, with its new yet familiar rhythms. Amen.

Reader • **Parent Take-Home** • Summer Year 1

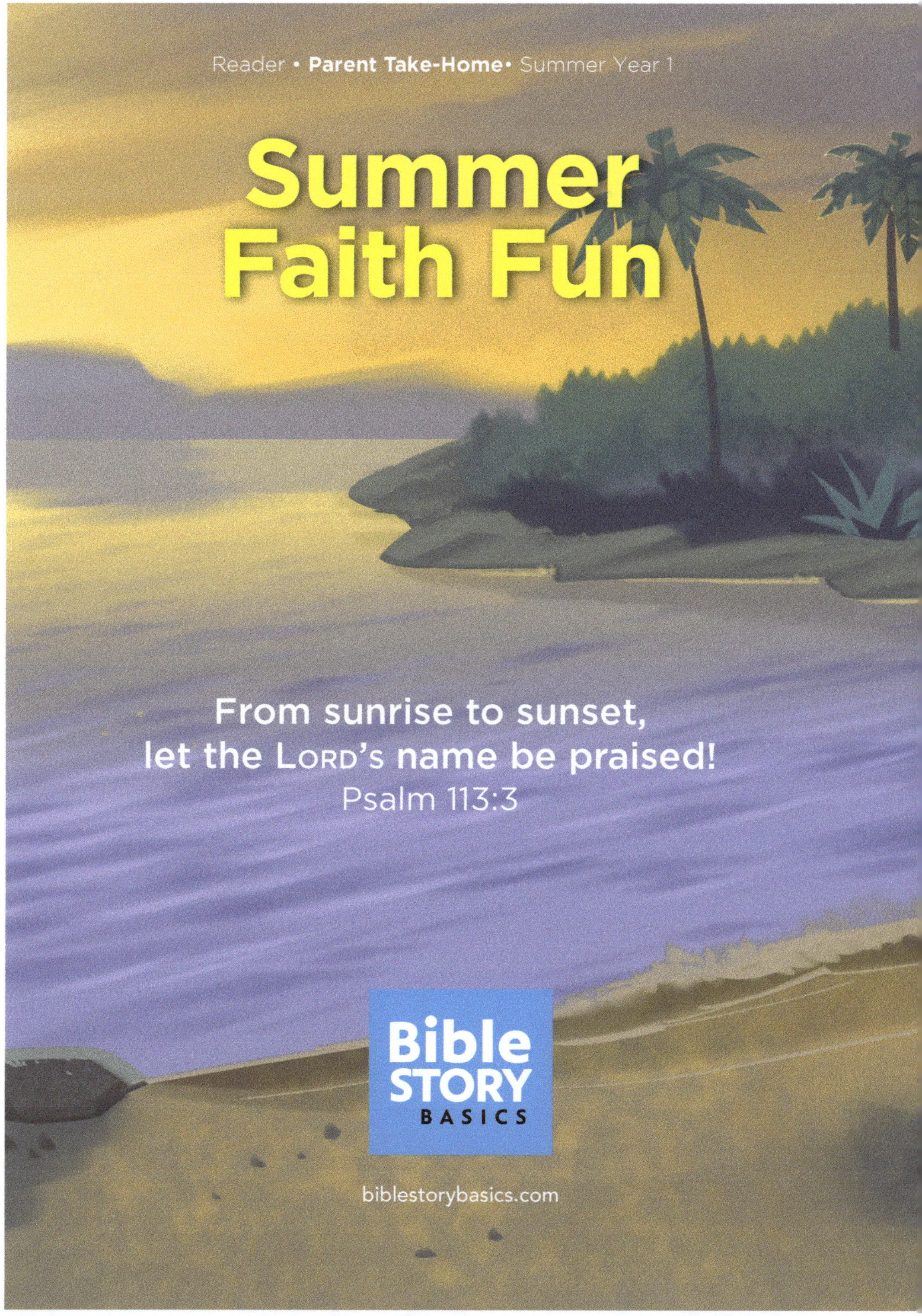

Summer Faith Fun

From sunrise to sunset,
let the LORD's name be praised!
Psalm 113:3

Bible STORY BASICS

biblestorybasics.com

Summer Spirituality

Ah, summer. Summer can be a season of rest and relaxation, constant activity and chaos, and spiritual renewal—all at the same time. Whether you spend your summer at the pool, at day camp, in the office, or traveling the world, the daily routines we count on shift. To some degree, everything feels different in the summer. As the tighter schedules and stressors of the school year relax, take some time to build new faith habits into your day. Here are some ideas for you to try with your children.

Track the sun's rise and set times. Watch how the days grow longer and longer until the summer solstice and then begin slowly to shorten through the remainder of summer. Each day when you check the "sun times" (or at sunrise and sunset if you witness them as a family), say a prayer together: "Lord Jesus, light of the world, shine in my heart and life today and every day."

Whether it's swimming in the neighborhood pool, jumping the waves at the beach, or watching a summer thunderstorm roll in, summer is full of water (even if our reservoirs are not). When you have a "water moment" with your family, pause and say a short prayer: "Thank you, God, for the life-giving gift of water. May the water remind us of the waters of baptism, and may we hear again the name you love to call us: your beloved children."

As you gather with friends, relatives, and neighbors, take a moment before eating to thank God for the abundance of summer foods and for your gathered community: "God, for the food before us, the people next to us, and the love among us, we give you thanks."

Enjoy your summer!

You've Got Mail!

Paul wrote letters to Christians in many cities. Starting from the center of the maze, help get Paul's letters to the churches in the different cities.

Talk About It

Use these questions to talk about today's Bible story with your child.

- Why do you think Paul wrote letters to the different churches?
- Who in your life helps you feel loved? What do these people do or say that shows you that they love you?

PRAY: Thank you, God, for your love, which is real and strong. Help us love others like you love us. Amen.

Love in Action

Romans 12:9-18

I can endure all these things through the power of the one who gives me strength.
Philippians 4:13

Bible STORY BASICS

biblestorybasics.com

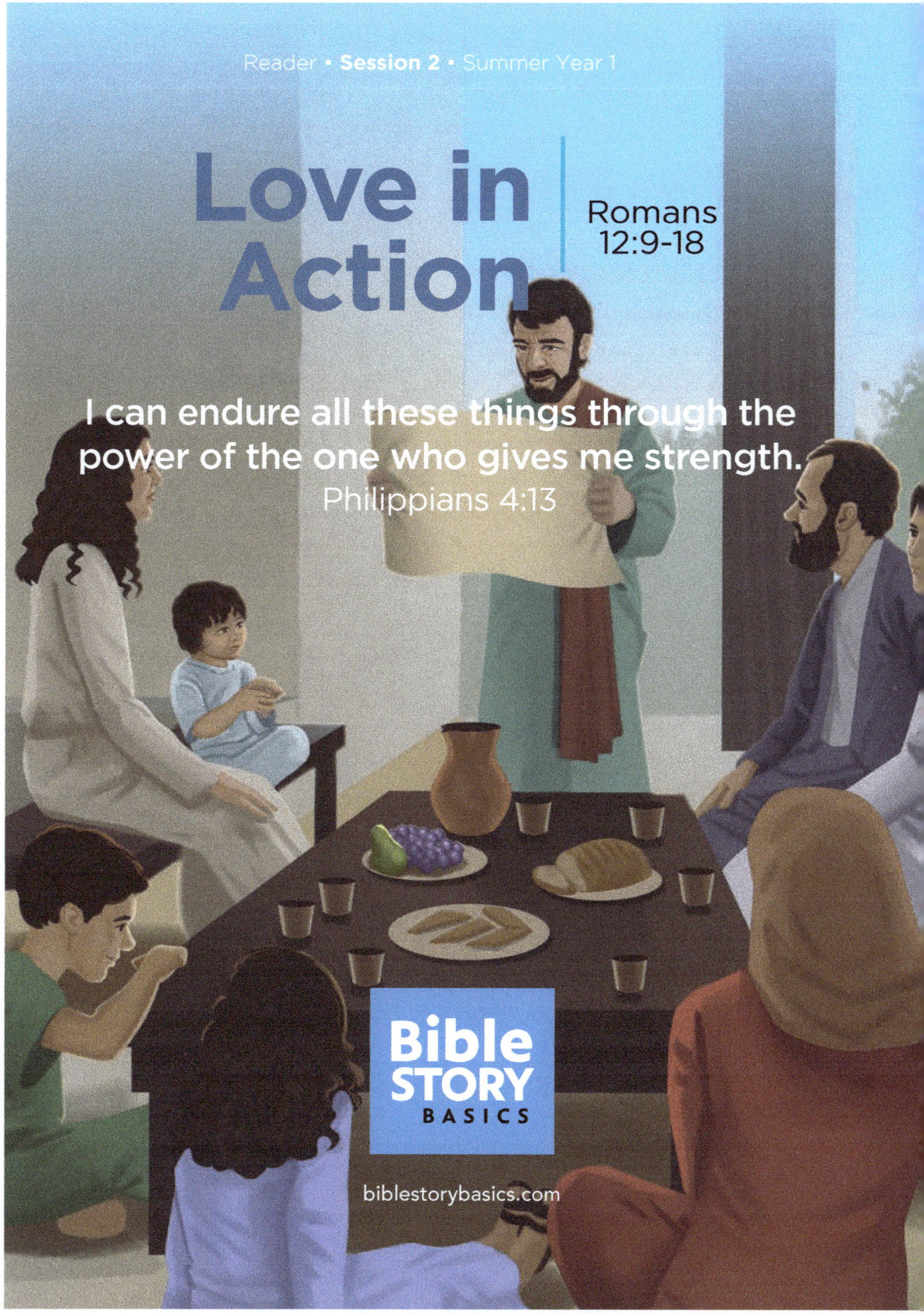

Love in Action

Dear _____ ,

_____
_____
_____
_____
_____
_____
_____

In Christ's Love,

_____

I Can Endure All Things

Find the words of the memory verse in the puzzle.

I	these	power	who
can	things	of	gives
endure	through	the	me
all	the	one	strength

Talk About It

Use these questions to talk about today's Bible story with your child.

- Do you think Paul was surprised that the Christians did not trust him? Why or why not?
- How do you decide whether or not to trust someone?

PRAY: God, give us wisdom to know who to trust. Thank you for always being trustworthy. Amen.

Reader • **Session 3** • Summer Year 1

Paul Escapes
Acts 9:20-25

I can endure all these things through the power of the one who gives me strength.
Philippians 4:13

Bible STORY BASICS

biblestorybasics.com

Paul Escapes

Should we trust Paul?

No	Yes

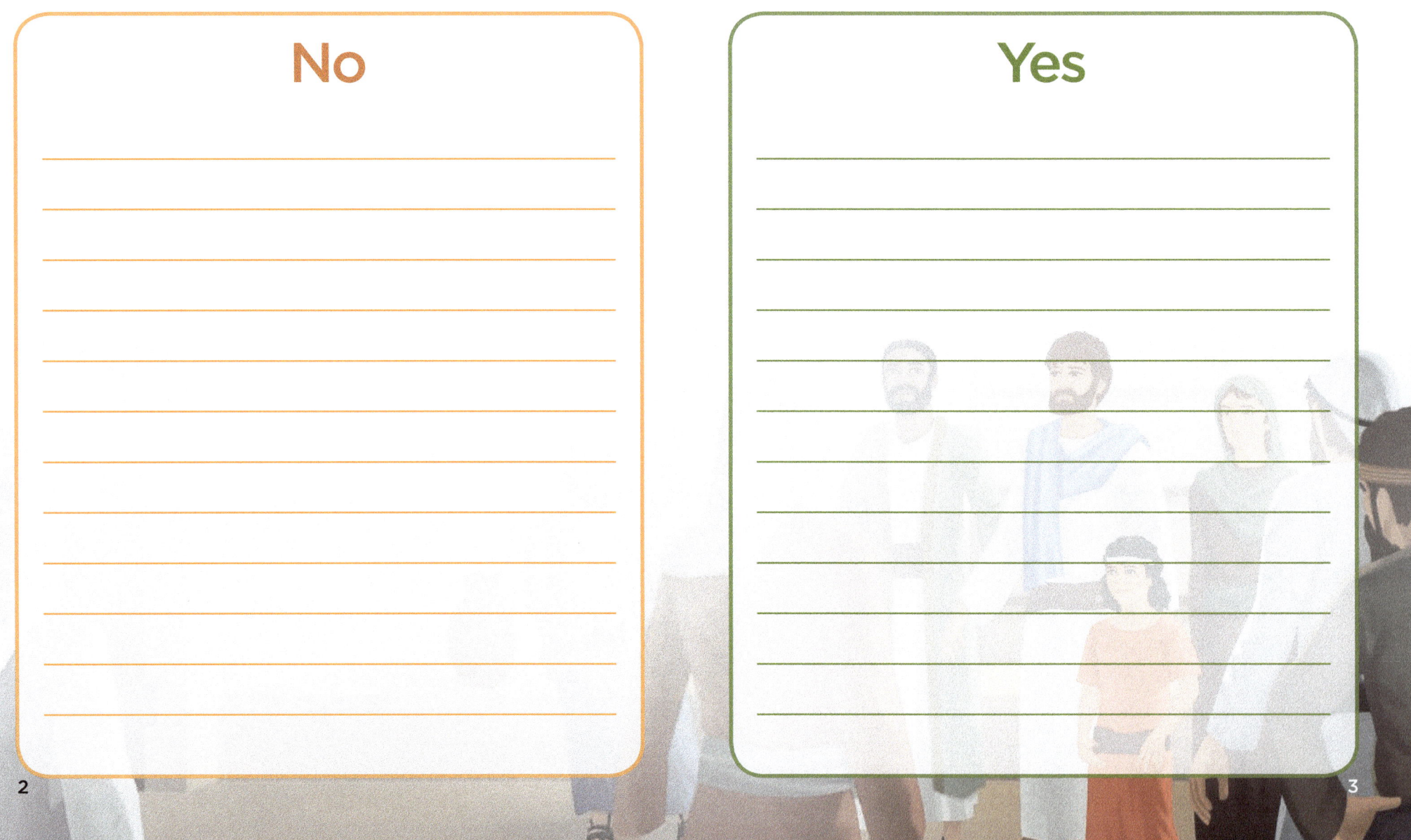

Peace

God gives us peace and the strength we need each day. To reveal the peace picture, color the R spaces red, Y spaces yellow, B spaces blue, O spaces orange, and G spaces green.

Talk About It

Use these questions to talk about today's Bible story with your child.

- What makes you anxious? What helps you feel calm?
- What are you grateful for?

PRAY: Dear God, thank you for giving us your peace, strength, joy, and endurance. Amen.

Reader • Session 4 • Summer Year 1

Be Glad and Endure
Philippians 4:4-14

I can endure all these things through the power of the one who gives me strength.
Philippians 4:13

biblestorybasics.com

Be Glad and Endure

Gratitude Journal

SUNDAY
1. _____
2. _____
3. _____
4. _____
5. _____

MONDAY
1. _____
2. _____
3. _____
4. _____
5. _____

TUESDAY
1. _____
2. _____
3. _____
4. _____
5. _____

WEDNESDAY
1. _____
2. _____
3. _____
4. _____
5. _____

THURSDAY
1. _____
2. _____
3. _____
4. _____
5. _____

FRIDAY
1. _____
2. _____
3. _____
4. _____
5. _____

SATURDAY
1. _____
2. _____
3. _____
4. _____
5. _____

Leadership

We can be leaders in many ways. Solve the puzzle to complete this sentence: We can be leaders through our __.

a c d e g h i l n
o p r s t u w y

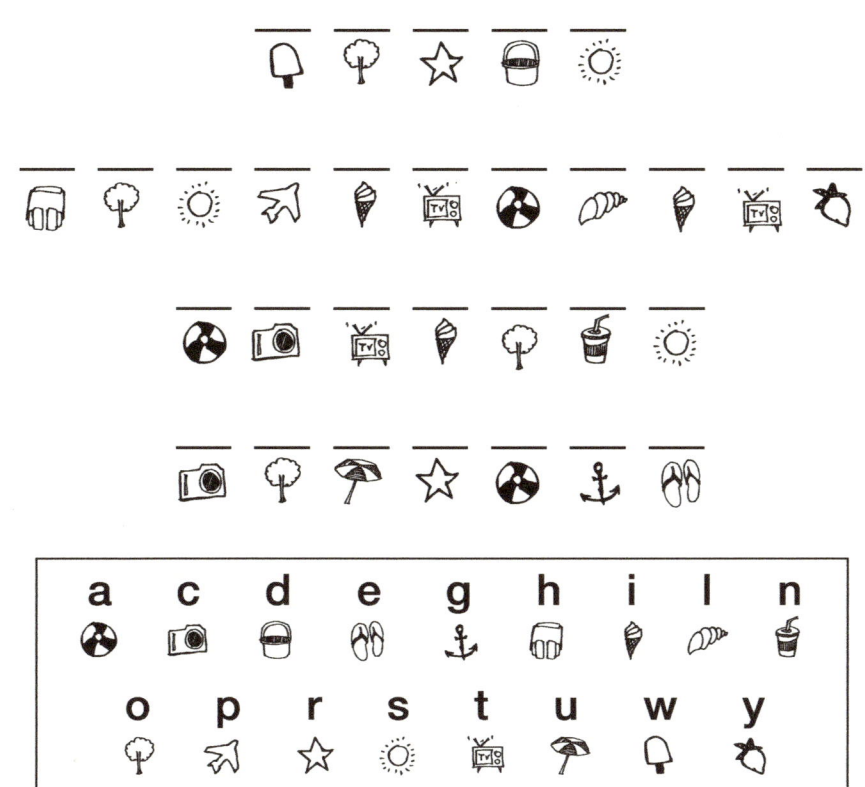

Talk About It

Use these questions to talk about today's Bible story with your child.

- Why do you think Paul chose Timothy to be a leader?
- How are you a leader in your life? What other opportunities can you take to lead?

PRAY: Dear God, help us take wise actions like Paul and Timothy did so that we can become leaders. Amen.

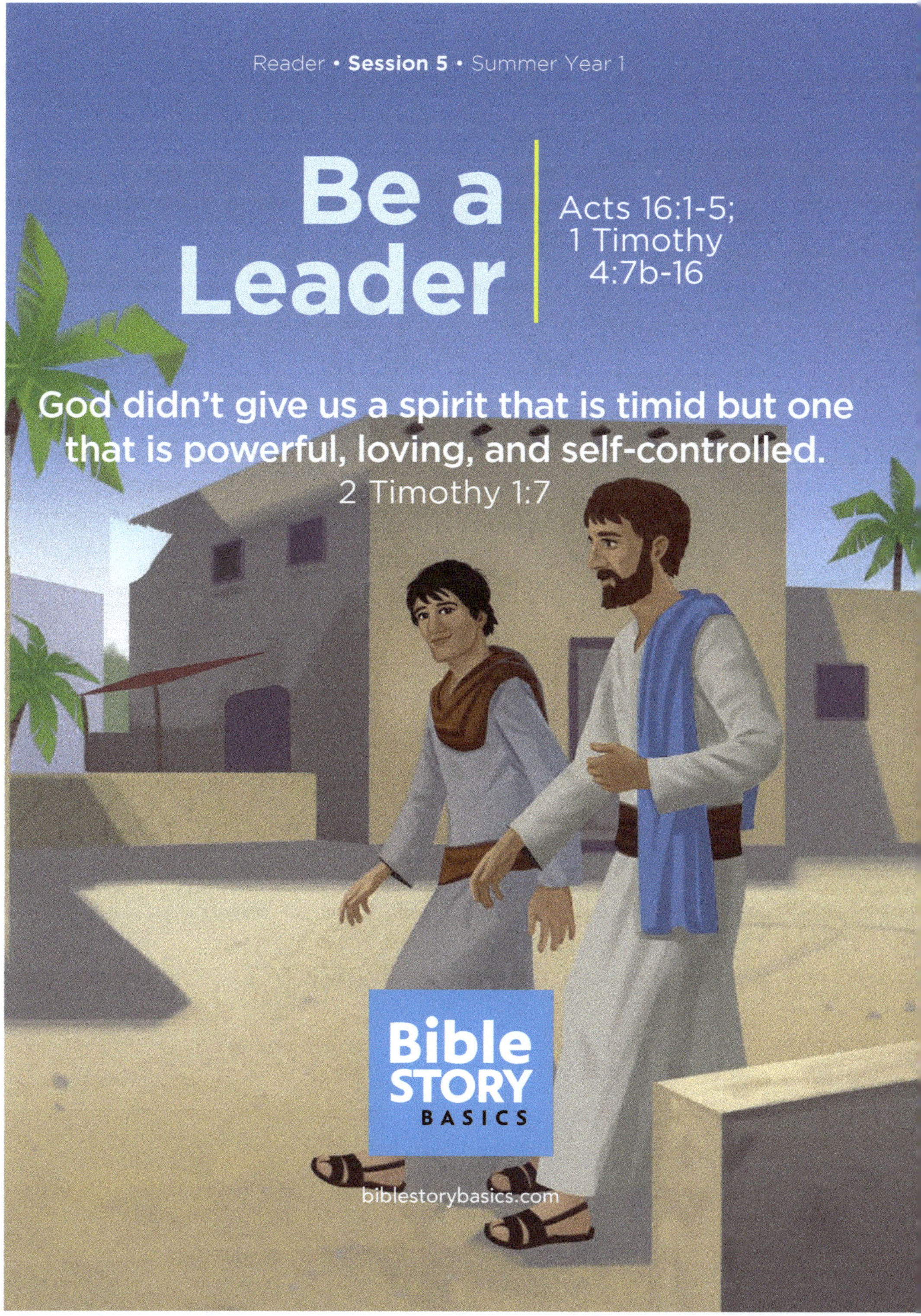
Reader • Session 5 • Summer Year 1
Be a Leader
Acts 16:1-5; 1 Timothy 4:7b-16
God didn't give us a spirit that is timid but one that is powerful, loving, and self-controlled.
2 Timothy 1:7
Bible STORY BASICS
biblestorybasics.com

Be a Leader

TOP TEN LIST FOR LEADERS

1. _____
2. _____
3. _____
4. _____
5. _____
6. _____
7. _____
8. _____
9. _____
10. _____

Building Up

Circle every third word to find the verse hidden in the puzzle.

Here in so joy house continue so that encouraging who was each inside road other those of and talk to building fruit of each Spirit wind other friend who up kind with just peace stay like sure comfort you but patient are make God doing live good already each other. (1 Thessalonians 5:11)

Talk About It

Use these questions to talk about today's Bible story with your child.

- What do you think it means to have a spirit that is powerful and loving?
- Who has helped you grow in your faith?

PRAY: Dear God, help us be leaders through our words by encouraging others. Amen.

Reader • Session 6 • Summer Year 1

Be Encouraged

2 Timothy 1:3-7

God didn't give us a spirit that is timid but one that is powerful, loving, and self-controlled.
2 Timothy 1:7

BIBLE STORY BASICS

biblestorybasics.com

Be Encouraged

Dear Paul,

_____

_____

_____

_____

_____

_____

_____

Your coworker in Christ,
Timothy

Down by the Riverside

Help Paul find his way to Lydia.

Talk About It

Use these questions to talk about today's Bible story with your child.

- Who are some of the faithful women leaders in your life?
- What does it mean to welcome someone? How do you welcome others into your home or church?

PRAY: Dear God, help us be leaders by welcoming others, like Lydia did. Amen.

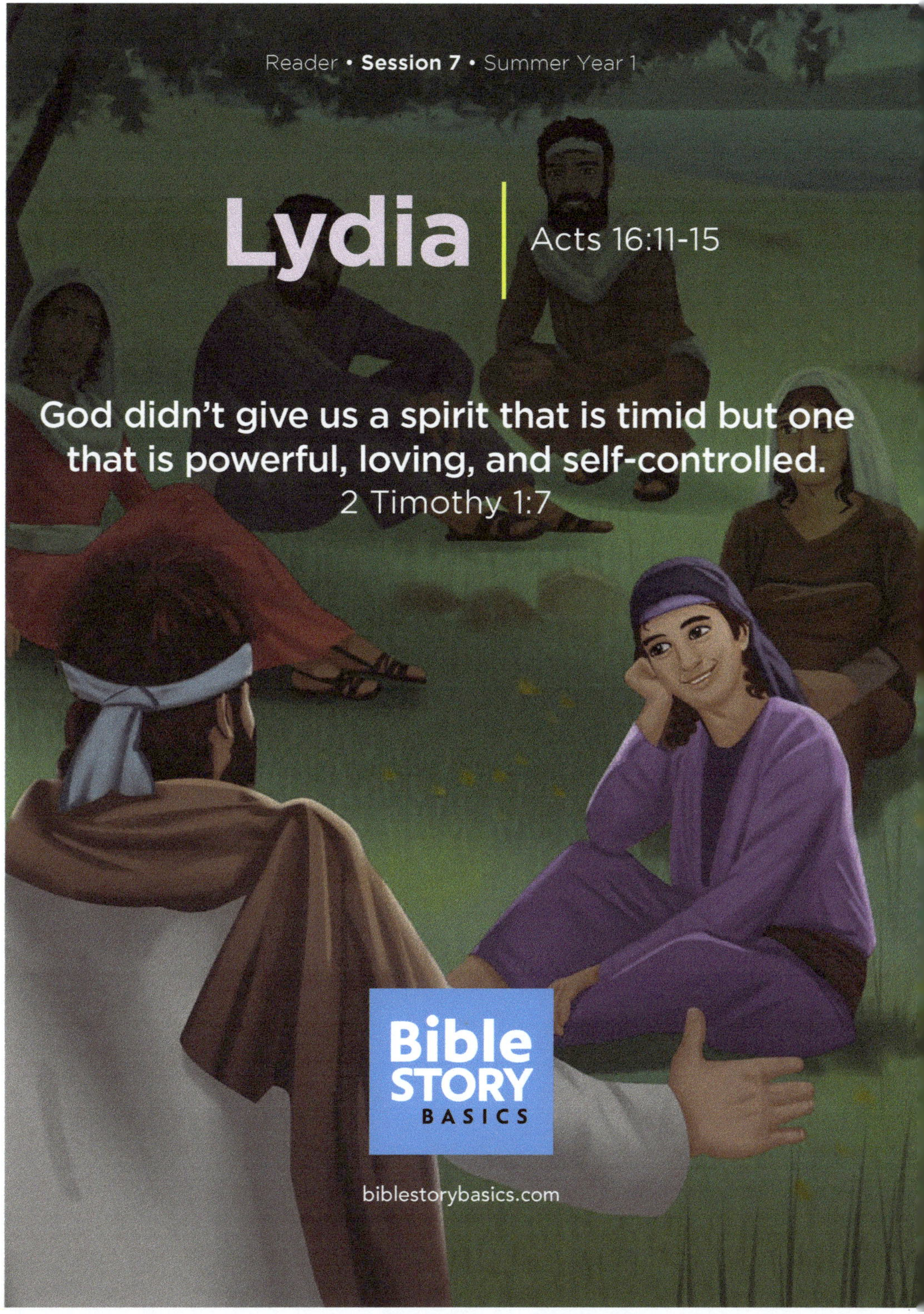

Lydia | Acts 16:11-15

God didn't give us a spirit that is timid but one that is powerful, loving, and self-controlled.
2 Timothy 1:7

Bible STORY BASICS

biblestorybasics.com

Lydia

Seen

Heard

Felt

Listen closely as the Bible story is read again. Pay attention to what Lydia might have seen, heard, felt, tasted, or smelled. Make notes in each box.

Tasted

Smelled

Jailbreak

Paul and Silas were locked in the jail. Can you find 10 keys hidden in the picture? After you have found the keys, color the picture.

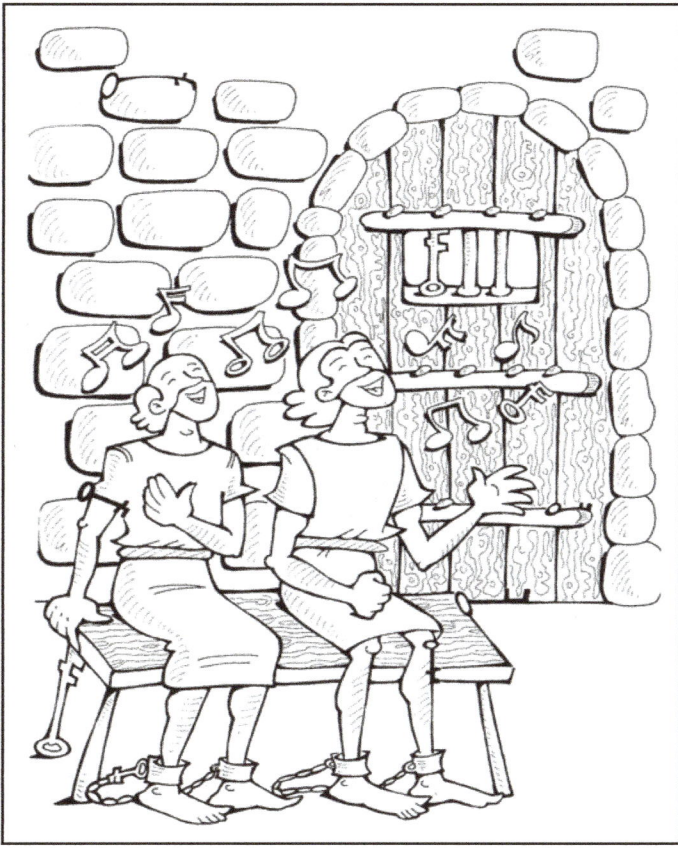

Talk About It

Use these questions to talk about today's Bible story with your child.

- Why do you think Paul and Silas didn't run away when the jail's doors flew open?
- Has someone ever gotten angry at you because of something you believed?

PRAY: Dear God, help us be leaders by being courageous. Amen.

Paul and Silas

Acts 16:16-40

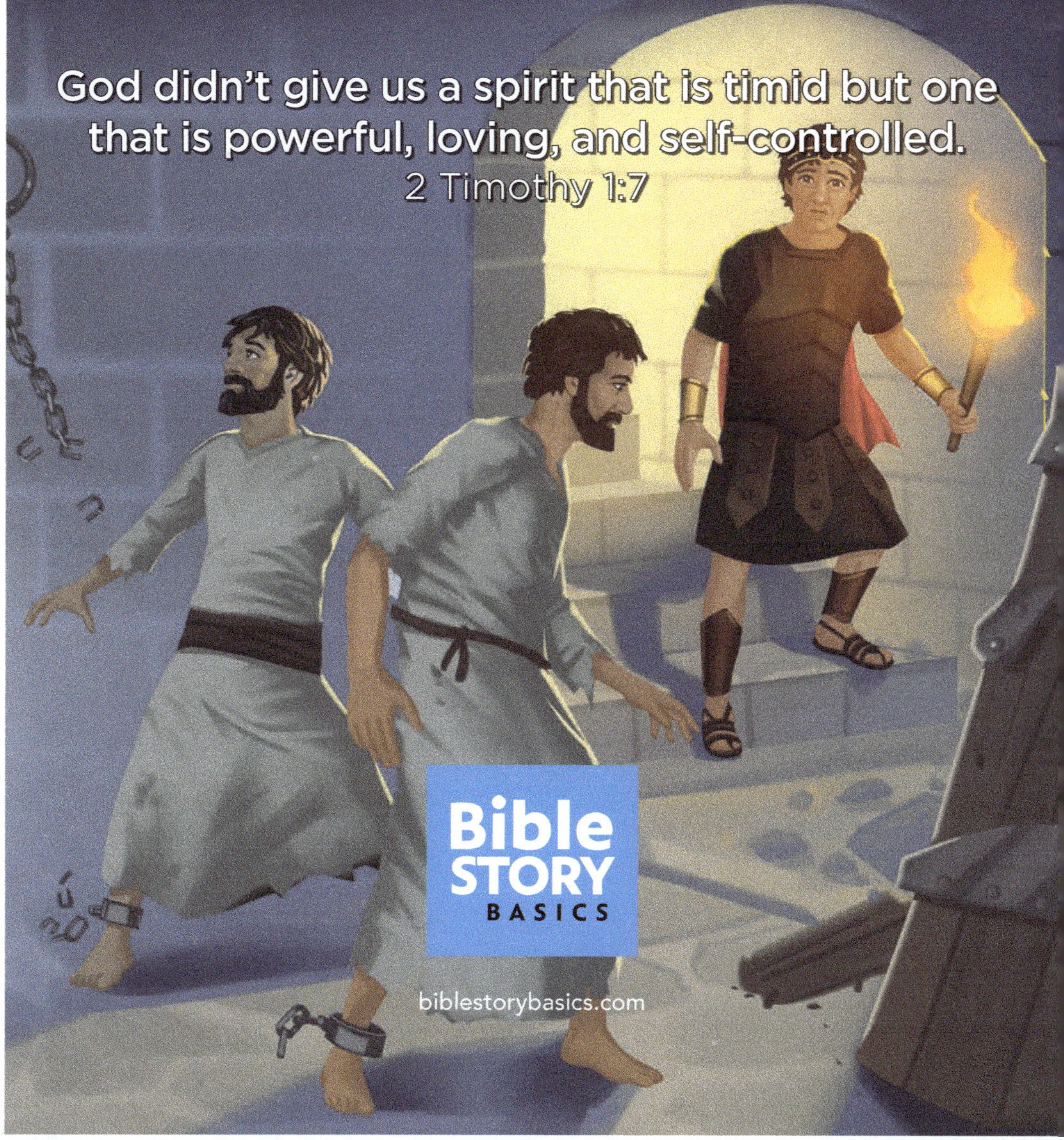

Paul and Silas

Characters: Paul, Silas, Crowd, Jailer, Jail (two people), Jailer's Family

Paul and Silas were followers of Jesus. They worked together to tell everyone they met about Jesus. *(Paul and Silas walk among the Crowd and shake everyone's hands.)*

Some people listened to Paul and Silas. *(Paul and Silas preach.)* Some of the people liked what Paul and Silas said. *(Some of the Crowd nod, smile, and look thoughtful.)* But some of the people did not want Paul and Silas to tell others about Jesus. *(Others in the Crowd look grumpy.)* These people said, "Send them to jail!"

Paul and Silas were put in jail. *(Jailer walks Paul and Silas to the Jail.)* Their hands and feet were chained to the wall. *(Jailer chains them to the wall. Jail stands behind Paul and Silas and holds their hands up.)* Paul and Silas were not sad. They prayed and sang songs to God. *(Paul and Silas sing and pray and dance while Jail holds their wrists.)*

Suddenly, the jail began to shake! It was an earthquake! *(Jail shakes.)* The chains on Paul and Silas fell off. The jail door swung open. *(Jail drops the wrists of* Paul and Silas *and swings open like a door.)*

"Oh, no!" said the jailer when he saw the open door. *(Jailer looks scared.)* "I'm sure all my prisoners ran away. I'll get in trouble for letting them go." *(Jailer shakes in fear.)*

"Don't worry!" said Paul. "Everyone is still here!" *(Jailer takes a deep breath and relaxes.)*

Then Paul and Silas told the jailer about Jesus. *(Paul and Silas preach again.)*

"I want to know more," said the jailer. "Come home with me and tell my family about Jesus." *(Jailer indicates that Paul and Silas should follow him. They walk to the Jailer's Family.)*

Paul and Silas told the jailer's whole family about Jesus. *(Paul and Silas preach again.)* The jailer and his family became followers of Jesus. *(Paul, Silas, Jailer, and Jailer's Family hold hands and pretend to pray.)*

Birds to the Rescue

Connect the dots to see the kind of birds that brought Elijah food.

Talk About It

Use these questions to talk about today's Bible story with your child.

- Have you ever felt as sad and alone as Elijah felt? When? What helped you feel better?
- Who helps take care of you, beyond your family?

PRAY: Dear God, thank you for teaching Elijah to trust you. Help us trust you too. Amen.

Reader • **Session 9** • Summer Year 1

Elijah and the Ravens

1 Kings 16:29-30; 17:1-7

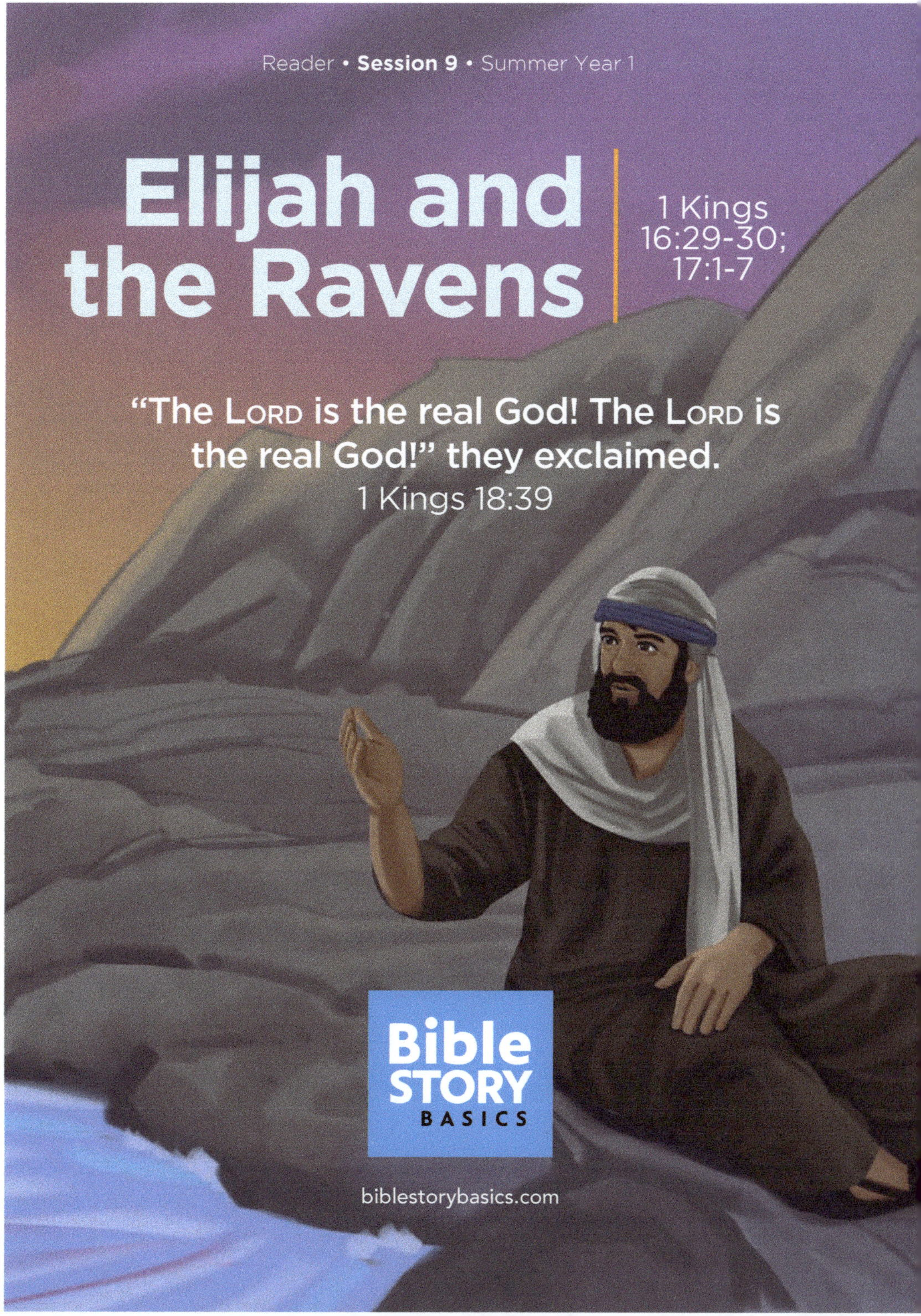

"The LORD is the real God! The LORD is the real God!" they exclaimed.
1 Kings 18:39

Bible STORY BASICS

biblestorybasics.com

Elijah and the Ravens

1. adjective
2. noun
3. name
4. adjective
5. noun
6. name
7. animal (plural)
8. verb
9. verb
10. noun
11. noun
12. verb
13. noun
14. noun
15. verb

God's Power

In order to show God's power, God made a fire on Elijah's altar. Add fire to this altar.

Talk About It

Use these questions to talk about today's Bible story with your child.

- Why do you think the prophets of Baal were so sure they would win?
- Think about a time you had to stand up for God or for yourself. What did you do? How did it feel?

PRAY: Dear God, thank you for giving Elijah the wisdom and courage to stand up for you. Help us to do so too. Amen.

Elijah and the Prophets
1 Kings 18:20-39

"The LORD is the real God! The LORD is the real God!" they exclaimed.
1 Kings 18:39

Elijah and the Prophets

| 1 Kings 18:20-21 | 1 Kings 18:22-24 | 1 Kings 18:25-26 | 1 Kings 18:27-29 |

| 1 Kings 18:30-35 | 1 Kings 18:36-37 | 1 Kings 18:38-39 |

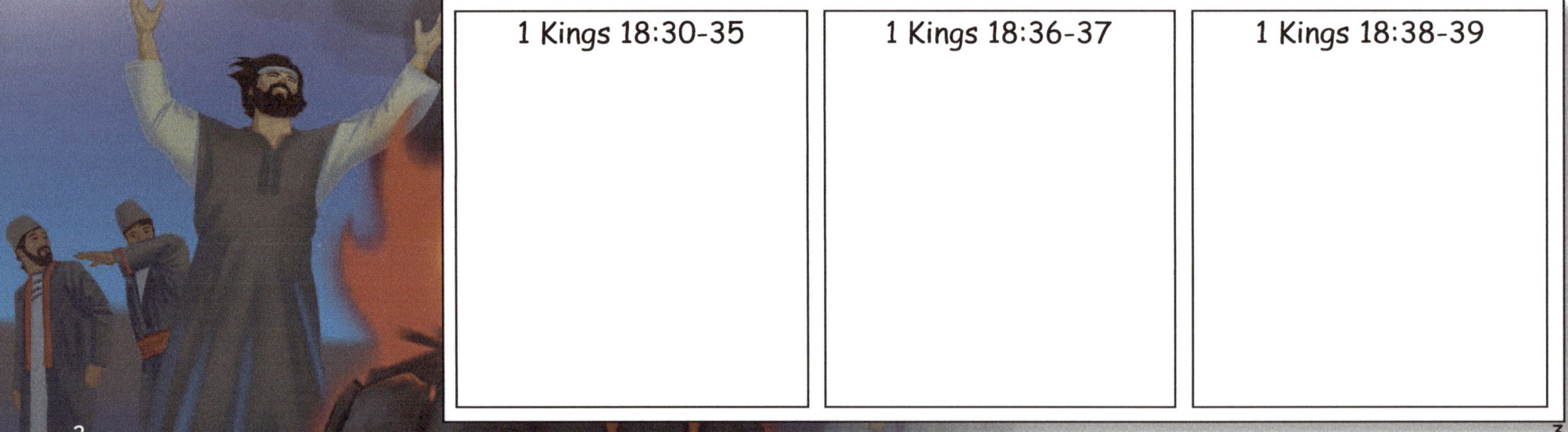

Jumbled-Up Story

The words from today's Bible story got all jumbled up by the whirlwind and the earthquake. Can you straighten them out?

_ _ _ _ _ NIDW

_ _ _ _ _ LABA

_ _ _ _ _ _ _ _ _ _ _ QKETEAHARU

_ _ _ _ _ _ _ ISAHLE

_ _ _ _ _ _ TUQIE

_ _ _ _ _ _ JEIAHL

_ _ _ _ ATCO

_ _ _ _ _ _ _ ZEEBJLE

_ _ _ _ _ _ _ HRPOPTE

Talk About It

Use these questions to talk about today's Bible story with your child.

- Elijah wanted Elisha to travel with him. How do you think Elisha felt about leaving his home?
- How do you listen for God's voice? How do you know when you hear God's voice?

PRAY: Dear God, thank you for giving Elijah the friend he needed to journey with him. Help us be that friend to someone. Amen.

Reader • Session 11 • Summer Year 1

Elijah and Elisha

1 Kings 19:1-21

"The Lord is the real God! The Lord is the real God!" they exclaimed.
1 Kings 18:39

Bible STORY BASICS

biblestorybasics.com

Elijah and Elisha

Characters: Narrator, God, Elijah, Elisha, Jezebel, Wind, Earthquake, Fire

Narrator: Elijah was afraid. *(Elijah looks afraid.)*

Elijah: *(shakily)* I'm…scared! Of her! *(Points to Queen Jezebel.)*

Jezebel: *(angrily)* You should be! You killed my prophets. And by the end of the day, I'll kill you!

(Elijah yelps and runs away.)

Narrator: Elijah ran for his life. He ran all the way to a cave. Now Elijah was sad. *(Elijah looks sad.)*

Elijah: *(pitifully)* I'm sad! And all alone!

Narrator: Elijah sat alone inside the cave. God saw Elijah in the cave.

God: *(from off-stage)* Elijah, why did you run away?

Elijah: I love you, but I am the only prophet left. This is super hard. They are trying to KILL me! I'm so sad. *(Elijah sobs.)*

God: Go out and stand at the mountain. Look alive! I will come by you.

Narrator: Elijah stood up and walked outside the cave. *(Elijah stands up and walks.)* Suddenly, a strong wind blew. *(Wind comes onstage and runs circles around Elijah.)* But God was not in the wind.

Narrator: An earthquake shook. *(Earthquake comes onstage and stomps around Elijah.)* But God was not in the earthquake.

Narrator: A fire burned. *(Fire comes onstage and dances around Elijah.)* But God was not in the fire. *(Wind, Earthquake, and Fire leave Elijah.)*

Narrator: Then everything became very still and very quiet. *(Pause. Everyone freezes. Slowly and silently, God approaches Elijah and stands next to him.)* God was in the quiet.

God: Elijah, I don't want you to be sad, alone, and afraid. Find a man named Elisha. He will be the next prophet.

Narrator: Elijah left the cave and found Elisha. *(Elijah walks over to Elisha.)*

Elijah: Elisha, God has told me that you will be the next prophet. Here, wear my prophet coat. *(Puts the coat on Elisha.)*

Elisha: *(surprised)* Me? Well, if God says so, I guess it's so! *(more confidently now)* This coat looks pretty good on me. Let's go!

Narrator: And so Elisha became the next prophet for God. *(Elijah and Elisha walk away together.)*

Hidden Pictures

Circle the objects that use oil. Then color the pictures.

Talk About It

Use these questions to talk about today's Bible story with your child.

- How do you think the woman felt when she couldn't pay the debts? How do you think she felt when all the jars were filled with oil?

- Have you ever worried you wouldn't have enough, but then you ended up with extra? How did it happen? How did you feel?

PRAY: Dear God, thank you for working through Elisha to help people. Work through us to help people too. Amen.

Elisha and the Widow
2 Kings 4:1-7

"The LORD is the real God! The LORD is the real God!" they exclaimed.
1 Kings 18:39

Bible STORY BASICS

biblestorybasics.com

Elisha and the Widow

Things have gone from bad to worse.

First, my dad died. Now it's just me, my mom, and my brother. It's awfully hard for a family in our culture to get by without a dad. My mom has been working hard and somehow getting us the food we need.

But then a man came. He said my dad owed him money. My mom told him that my dad had died and she didn't have the money. How could she come up with that much money?

The man didn't care. He said that a debt was a debt. It didn't matter that my dad had died. The debt didn't die.

"That's not fair!" I almost shouted. But my mom gave me a look that clearly said, "Be quiet!" I kept my mouth shut, but I didn't like it. And the man wasn't exactly kind to my mom. Before he left, he said that if she didn't come up with the money, he would come back and take me and my brother away as slaves.

I was NOT going to go anywhere with him. I wasn't going to leave my mom or my little brother. My mom was upset and didn't know what to do.

She heard that the prophet Elisha was in town, so she asked him for advice. He told us to go around the village and collect as many jars as we could. Now our house is full of jars!

My mom kept filling the jars from our tiny jar of oil. It was the weirdest thing—that tiny jar didn't run empty until all the jars were filled!

I don't know how all of this is going to end, but I know that this much oil costs a lot of money. Surely it will be enough to pay off the debt so that we can stay together. After all, it's just me, my mom, and my brother against the world. Well, with Elisha too.

Who Can God Help?

Find the missing letter in each row and write it on its corresponding line. The word will answer the question "Who can God help?"

1. A B C D F G H I J K L M N O P Q R S T U V W X Y Z
2. A B C D E F G H I J K L M N O P Q R S T U W X Y Z
3. A B C D E F G H I J K L M N O P Q R S T U V W X Y Z
4. A B C D E F G H I J K L M N O P Q S T U V W X Y Z
5. A B C D E F G H I J K L M N O P Q R S T U V W X Z
6. A B C D E F G H I J K L M N P Q R S T U V W X Y Z
7. A B C D E F G H I J K L M O P Q R S T U V W X Y Z
8. A B C D F G H I J K L M N O P Q R S T U V W X Y Z

___ ___ ___ ___ ___ ___ ___ ___
 1   2   3   4   5   6   7   8

Talk About It

Use these questions to talk about today's Bible story with your child.

- Naaman assumed it would be hard to be healed of his skin disease. Why do you think Elisha had Naaman do something as simple as washing in the river to be healed?

- What do you do when you encounter someone different from you who needs help? Do the differences make you nervous?

PRAY: Dear God, thank you for loving and helping everyone, no matter our differences. Help us love and help everyone. Amen.

Reader • **Session 13** • Summer Year 1

Elisha and Naaman
2 Kings 5:1-19a

"The LORD is the real God! The LORD is the real God!" they exclaimed.
1 Kings 18:39

Bible STORY BASICS

biblestorybasics.com

Elisha and Naaman

I'm an important general in the army, but I can't stop itching! Please help me!

Who am I? _____

I have an idea! There's a prophet near my home who can help.

Who am I? _____

Dear, please take the journey and see if you can be cured. It's time you were made well!

Who am I? _____

I value Naaman's leadership. If he needs to take this journey, I'll send money and supplies with him.

Who am I? _____

What do I know about healing skin diseases? I'm a king, for goodness sake!

Who am I? _____

My God is so strong and mighty that I don't even have to touch Naaman for him to be healed.

Who am I? _____

Sure, my job isn't flashy, but I'm happy to serve a prophet of the Lord.

Who am I? _____

We're tired of hearing about the itching. Sure, it sounds miserable, but enough is enough. We'll help Naaman try anything to be healed. Anything.

Who are we? _____

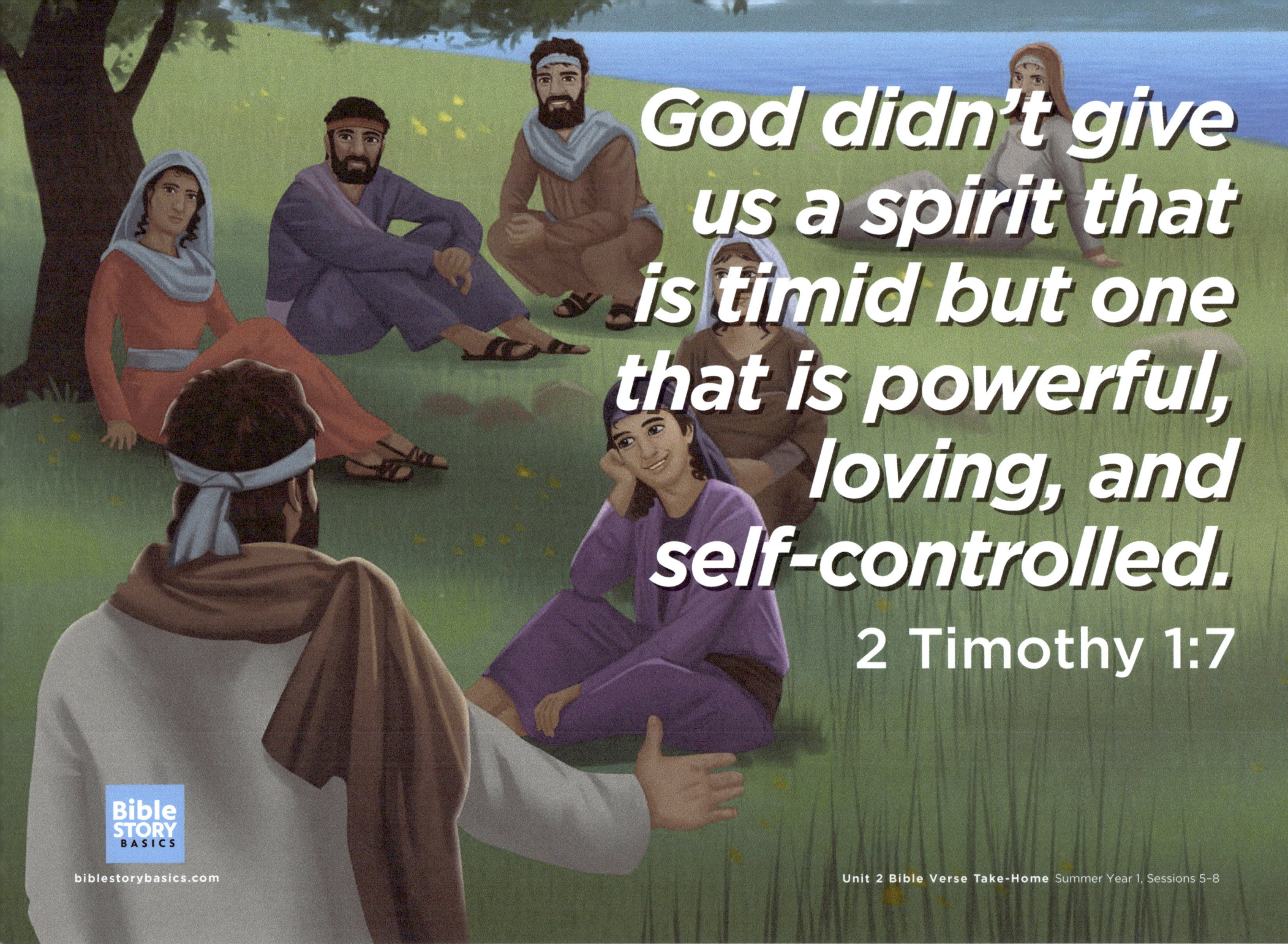

Vol. 1 • No. 4 • Summer Year 1

EDITORIAL / DESIGN TEAM

Nancy Speas	Writer
Brittany Sky	Editor
Heidi Hewitt	Production Editor
Jim Carlton	Designer

ADMINISTRATIVE TEAM

Rev. Brian K. Milford	President and Publisher
Marjorie M. Pon	Associate Publisher and Editor of Church School Publications
Mary M. Mitchell	Design Manager
Brittany Sky	Senior Editor, Children's Resources

Bible Story Basics: Reader, Bible Story Leaflets: An official resource for The United Methodist Church approved by Discipleship Ministries and published quarterly by Abingdon Press, a division of The United Methodist Publishing House, 2222 Rosa L. Parks Blvd., Nashville, TN 37228-1306. Price: $8.99. Copyright © 2020 Abingdon Press. All rights reserved. Send address changes to Bible Story Basics: Reader, Bible Story Leaflets, Subscription Services, 2222 Rosa L. Parks Blvd., Nashville, TN 37228-1306 or call 800-672-1789. Printed in China.

To order copies of this publication, call toll free: **800-672-1789**. You may fax your order to 800-445-8189. Telecommunication Device for the Deaf/ Telex Telephone: 800-227-4091. Or order online at *cokesbury.com*. Use your Cokesbury account, American Express, Visa, Discover, or Mastercard.

For information concerning permission to reproduce any material in this publication, write to Rights and Permissions, The United Methodist Publishing House, 2222 Rosa L. Parks Blvd., Nashville, TN 37228-1306. You may fax your request to 615-749-6128. Or email *permissions@umpublishing.org*.

Scripture quotations unless noted otherwise are taken from the Common English Bible, copyright 2011. Used by permission. All rights reserved.

Cover design by Ed Maksimowicz. Illustrations by Ralph Voltz. Art: pp. 1, 2, & 3 of Sessions 1–13, Unit 1 Bible Verse Take-Home, Unit 2 Bible Verse Take-Home, Unit 3 Bible Verse Take-Home: Ralph Voltz. p. 4 of Sessions 1–2, 4–5, 7–10, 12: Four Story Creative, Thinkstock, Shutterstock, Cokesbury curriculum, and Abingdon curriculum, Bible Library Take-Home: Jim Carlton.

PACPI0557320-01